Comprehen... ...ever

Willow Books

Detroit, Michigan

Comprehending Forever

Copyright © 2014 by Rich Villar

Editor: Randall Horton
Cover art: "TREGUA" by Dafne Elvira

ISBN 978-0-9897357-5-9

Willow Books, a Division of Aquarius Press
PO Box 23096
Detroit, MI 48223
www.WillowLit.net

Printed in the United States of America

Dedication

This list will come up short. I apologize in advance.

Thank you—

To the family at Willow Books/Aquarius Press: Heather Buchanan-Gueringer and Randall Horton. Your work is needed. To the judges of the Willow Books Literature Awards: Naomi Ayala, Ching-In Chen, and John Murillo. Thank you for seeing me.

A mi familia: Mom, Pop, Christina and Robert, Gus and Dawn. Forever started with you. Because you believed, I believed. I love you all.

To Martín Espada: Thank you, Maestro, for your steady and uncompromising friendship. For your grace and strength. For your guidance, and for guarding our honor. Your students refuse surrender.

To Willie Perdomo: you taught me how to be fearless, and you taught me what it is to say brother and mean it. For real.

To Luivette Resto: My twin sister, my homegirl, the co-star of my very own Latino Lifetime TV movie. You know the stories, and you helped write them. Thank you, Lulu, for being the Ephron to my Reiner.

To the Revolutionaries: Antonio, Sofia, and Joaquín. I can't wait to play another round of 20,000 Questions with you.

To Maria Nieves-Stevens: The sister I never asked for, and got anyway, who saw me turn into a writer, who never forgets to let me know what I'm worth when I don't seem to know. Thank you. My mother still calls you Millybakes.

To Alexa Muñoz: Your resilience astonishes me. I don't tell you enough how much you are loved and respected like a sister, so I chose the biggest stage I could to say you're amazing. And that your students are unbelievably blessed.

To Natalia Agüeros-Macario: Thank you, sister, for your ear, your heart, the lessons in being a guardian, a good steward, and a better friend. Thanks for the talks and texts, and for the tower of shoeboxes, of course.

To Oscar Bermeo: You have coaxed me out of so many different shells over the years. Thank you for your brotherhood, friendship, and truthfulness. And thank you for *Acentos*.

To John Rodriguez; and Chino Suarez, Luis "Bundy" Medina, John Medina, Robert Brown, Adrian Morene, Cindy Taverez, Fabiola Paredes, and all the poets of the

Whedco Teen Program, 168th Street, Morrisania, South Bronx. Many things are true at once. I am always here.

Thank you Acentos. Thank you Cave Canem, Cantomundo, and Kundiman. Thank you to my workshop at Bread Loaf: James Longenbach, Jeanette Anderson, Charles Byrne, Christine Gosnay, Richie Hofmann, Jude Kelly, Linda Martin, Elizabeth Onusko, Margaret Ross, and Philip Williams.

Thank you to my friends and extended family from every corner of every world I have ever inhabited, where poetry became real: Lynne Procope, Roger Bonair-Agard, Patrick Rosal, Guy LeCharles Gonzalez, Abena Koomson, Elana Bell, Jai Chakrabarti, Mara Jebsen, Eric Guerreri, F. Omar Telan, Ed Garcia, Raymond Daniel Medina, Tish Valles, Corrina Bain, James Merenda, John Paul Davis, Bonafide Rojas, Mundo Rivera, Juan "Paposwiggity" Santiago, George Torres, Vincent Toro, Grisel Acosta, Cristina Velez, Jessica Torres, Raina Leon, Jessica Elizabeth Nadler, Matthew Charles Siegel, Kyra Wolfe, Juan Diaz, Jonaki Sanyal, Danny Solis, Robert Karimi, Vanessa Mártir, Vasialys Solae Mártir Rodriguez, Bianca Martinez, Soleil Feliz, Vanessa Acevedo, Glendaliz Camacho, Karen Rossi, Vallerie Matos (two L's!), Peggy Robles-Alvarado, Jorge Alvarado, Jaime Emeric, George Acevedo, Albert Areizaga, Viviann "True" Rodriguez, Adrienne Rodriguez, Maria Rodriguez, Nancy Arroyo Ruffin, Jamie Ricalde, Alicia Anabel Santos, Maria Corporan, Terry Becerril, Nia Andino, Anamaria Flores, Blanca Vega, John S. Blake, Mimi Blake, Laurie Ann Guerrero, Dan Vera, Urayoán Noel, LiYun Alvarado, Tony Brown, Maria Serrano, Sandra Dias-Rodriguez, Cess Oliva, Lisa Alvarado, Alison Hedge Coke, Margaret Porter-Troupe, Quincy Troupe, Cris Macario, Jeremy Stevens, Barbara Jane Reyes, Andre B. Black, Lauren Schmidt, Patricia Smith, Dennis Nurkse, Nancy Morejón, Jack Agüeros, Afaa M. Weaver, and Rod Hosterman, my first poetry teacher.

. . .] put them down, all their hawks
& quiet weeds, look those long days in the eyes,
see their sleepless flash & royal,
the hard, hard suffocating days, the days you danced in
wildly, even in your sleep. Here. & do not ever say again
that you don't know what it is to stay
or to be stayed with, that you don't get love
& maybe couldn't do it, not like that,
when, in fact, that's all you've ever known. Day
after day, after day, here is your love, your love
that has gone nowhere away from you...

~Aracelis Girmay, "Here"

Contents

Ars Poetica

Comprehending

for Dooley and Miriam

at night, you chase the sunrise.
at daybreak, you covet the brightening moon.

every eight minutes, the sun
ignites and extinguishes
every sacred point and holy
city in every world you know
and those you don't.

you are already dead.
you are already born again.

be still, Amor.

God desires passage,
and you are her compass.

Nightfall

Bop: First Meeting
with lyrics from Country Livin' (The World I Know), *by Esthero*

The treads of my shoes do not grip the sidewalk.
My hands are heavy. My hands remember
the cold glass, the swirling, *I have to go.*   All of her inhaled
in one cool breath.   Love is another word for walking away.
Rain standing on my skin. You have to go.
I smile anyway.

The world I know is a world much too slow.
If you can't move fast enough, child,
better stay on the low, child.

What do I do with this rain? Collect it
from my face. Hang it in a tree on Simpson Street.
I want you without dial tones to distract me.
Don't be distracted.
The moon rises and drives south along the river.
I want to be loved on my feet.
Love me with no red lights.
We have written this book already.

The world I know is a world much too slow.
If you can't move fast enough, child,
better stay on the low, child.

I don't know which direction your house is. Not sure I want to.
I want to point to Puerto Rico in June.
Dip my toes in Luquillo water.
Ours is slow method, moongirl. I will come to you
with head low, 3am, insomnia,
perfect Bustelo, Night, bridge, city lights.

The world I know is a world much too slow.
If you can't move fast enough, child,
better stay on the low, child.

November

waxing crescent

She loves me in Chinatown, five dollars from the moongirl's hand
to an old woman selling respite from rain. I guard her lips,
strong coffee in a cup, something suede. How she cradles
the weight of me in her hands. How she ends me:
seven long times under subway bench, F train, her moving muses.

waxing gibbous

She loves me in the rain, but only because she's under my umbrella.
Paterson is not Corcovado, and the E train is not El Yunque,
and I am more a rum person than a wine person. But I will brownbag
grapes from Argentina, because Stan Getz is a Jersey boy at heart,
and will hold her for the whole 15 blocks, shield her lips from drowning.

full

water across five smooth stones, sweat beading.
cuatro in my trained hands.   niña en la costa
de mi cariño, quiero olvidarme de que soy marino.
merlot fingers on double strings, resonating.
she never needed rum to see me. only hands.

waning gibbous

She loves me because chance has an address. We could have found out
about Corcovado at a marble table on 11th and 6th. I could have used it
as subterfuge to brush her hand with mine. The radio could have started
playing it, and we could have laughed. We could have watched wonder
creep across our faces in Portuguese. We could have walked home.

waning crescent

She loves me because sunset is Yunque grey, fire and rain.
The bay of Luquillo is a kaleidoscope. Aquamarine veil lowered

across our eyes. Here, I wrote my first words. Here, the sonnets start at your waistline. When I speak, the moon rises. Every sunset is a beach I want to write your name in.

Sonnet for a Waistline

I call it *la costa de mi cariño*:
name for summer, border, home
Olvidando de que soy yo marino.
My hand is eager, my skin, my bones

sue for sustenance. Running my fingers
through zen garden, tracing your hips
and collarbone, the scent of rain lingers
from belly to spine to heel to lips

to home. Your waist, a salve, a healing
concoction soothing tightness from chest.
The soundtrack is Corcovado. The ceiling,
a map to a rain forest. This bed, our test.

Praise to your navel, deconstructing time,
Praise to your waist, the perfection of wine.

Serenade: Arrival

I am low slung stone under full moon.
You are a giant contemplating jazz.

If I say to you I will not lie, it does not mean
the end of you is near. My arm
lowers to the ground. You are flinching.

I have forgotten my name because my stone
is a song drenched in Malbec.
Drink slowly, roll it in your mouth.

There are five stones, smooth like this one,
waiting for the orders to slip
beneath your waters,
and lie there until I call them forth again,
like a breath entering and exiting.

Kiss

I knew
a lily would open
to Corcovado
I knew
my hand would find
proper rest
at the bend of your hips
I knew
blood would rush
when a man
faces the death
of his old life
I knew
righteousness
flooded our sinuses
your breath and mine
a silent prayer ascending
I knew
I would worship
the death of clocks
no fear
no stoplights
I knew
death would wait
and claim another
not named the moon
I knew
no other hands
but mine and yours
mine and yours
mine and yours
I knew
my eyes would open
eager to drink
my first wine
I knew

understanding
a steel spine
beneath my fingers
chasing all the air
out of the room
I knew
the open wound
of my heart sealing
under our heat
I knew
the last drop
of summer's honey
on my tongue
could not match
what I tasted
in your kitchen
I knew
what takes fifty years
to properly say
she is not yours to solve
she is only the moon
shifting dark to pearl
to crescent walks home
understands
what you do not
fills art with need
wavering and returning
balance to your middle ear
I knew
lips caressing lips
could only happen
in a slow approach
a closing of space
our hearts were ready
to embrace
I knew
your voice
could end me
(it did)
I knew

your voice
could save me
(it did)
I knew
my voice
but never really knew
my voice
until you said

I knew. I always knew.

Only Now
after Philip Levine's "Call It Music"

You don't like when I bring things back to you,
but this is what happens when you are the moon.
We are sitting in a parked car in Jackson Heights,
the playground's muted green settling into sunset,
and now I wonder what color your panties are.
While discussing Levis' "Those Graves In Rome,"
openly fantasizing about visiting Rumi's tomb
in a country where no one calls him by that name,
suddenly you say "red," and there is no one alive
now, or in the deep breaths which follow. Only you,
beneath this city-funded street lamp, regal,
lit, the way photographers used to light
Grace Kelly. Years later, or tomorrow,
I will suggest that your breath on my neck is medicine,
is peace, depending on the hour of your coffee—
8am, 11pm, in a fishnet bodysuit, or pink flannel.
I am in mourning, or in love, depending
on answers I am unprepared to hear:
How does grace spring between these bricks?
How does God drop Stan Getz's saxophone
into my trembling hands?
How do we kiss through sleepless Wednesdays?
How do I find a face in your lifeline?
My heart is a distressed compass.
You cannot command it. I cannot lead you
into my dream. Only now
can I pour cherry wine over everything you ever doubted,
and drink it completely.

saying

my tongue,
a dark blue brush.

i won't stop
until you say
                too much

distance between shorelines,
or rivers of sugar.
will you say

this is foolish,
or yes, or yes
until the sun fills you?

will you say
forever the way you say
autopsy,

the way you say no,
or now?

Transgression
after Dorianne Laux

It is a slow kiss climbing, then descending.
It is a slow eye closing behind your navel.
I marvel at your abdomen quivering,
a congregation of neurons crashing against shoreline
of your waist. I am playing the cuatro again,
the notes resonating in my fingers. Choirs
raise their hands to God, who you have already called
once. I am breathing poems into your neck.
You breathe a book back into the air, pages burning,
rising and falling in Spanish:
Ay, Papi.
Te necesito.
Así, mi Amor.
Si, Papi.
Mamita, no te apures,
tenemos la noche entera.
And we do have the entire night, two spines,
Two spines, collarbones, your breasts against
my chest, fingertips and slow grind,
bundle of pulses, heartbeat keeping time,
lips and tongue and lungs in symphony.
Slow down, slow down.
You want me, this second, in ten seconds.
On Bleecker. Where you first imagined a saxophone.
Where you leaned your body into mine and said,
Let me go.
Let me practice the art of enactment tonight.
The letting go, the meandering tongue.
Let me have you in plain sight.
Let me lift you toward heaven,
in our time, in bossa novas,
dawn creeping up on us like a held note.

Turning

I am a city with blurred edges.

You are five thousand diamonds
spread across black velvet.

Last night, I flew above myself,
into the place where cold becomes steam
becomes you. I am washed clean
each morning in an updraft of exhales,

and I say,
I am not the brother, breathless, in the ground.
I am not the sister, breathless, in the ground.
I am not the husband, breathless, in the ground,

turning.

I am turning my face to the moon.
I am the avenue, you are a hawk, perched.
This is a nest.
This is your word for honesty.

My father gave me a map.

I found you standing in a field of Easter lillies
someone had planted in the center of the city.
The edges are medicine, are sleep.

Tonight, I am breath.
Tonight, I am your breath,
the wisp of steam beneath your pillow.

Answer

You greet me in my sleep.
You say: Remove the coins pressed against your eyes.
Wake up, guess where I'm going.

You are standing at Rumi's tomb.
Your lips, the red flesh of grapefruit.
Your hair, a river flowing north.
Your hips, an imagined banquet.

You wonder which open hands moved me to bless the field.
You wonder how I found the time.

There are no clocks in my book, and if there were,
I would curse them like sour wine.

Your left foot shifts.
My ring finger greets your middle toe.

I write this down. I pray:

Lord, who has given me red grapefruit,
Lord, who stirs the breath of deserts with her toes,
send her the answer she has known since childhood:

You are the edge of the roof, the field beyond.
You are my two insomnias, sun, raindrops, clouds, and sun.
You are the moon in the window.

You are the flood of nourishment. Overwhelmed.
The wave that carried me, despite my feet.

You are the muse, the breath,
the fingers, the poem.

Last Train

We are not home yet.

There are too many dark tunnels between here
and a bed from which all fear is banished.

You are always somewhere between Queens and Brooklyn.

I have a shirt with an S on the chest. It's my favorite.
Rescue is in my nature. I have resisted the urge
to fly into the hurricane and pluck you from the water.
So far.

I am not home yet because I can't fly home.
There is no rescue from the hurricane, I am terrible
at automobile maintenance, the trains stop running after 4.

Or, I was not ready to be saved first.

I was not ready for Technicolor Oz. I was not ready
for red curtains to dazzle at first light. I was not ready
for first light, morning coffee, a kiss that set me weeping.

The baby is asleep in the next room. She is your first light.
She will want for nothing so long as you remember this.

Which is to say: rise from the water, precious moon, rise
like the first kiss trembling in your technicolor dreamscape.
Everything I've ever wanted is shaped like your lips.

Even gypsies come home.

I have seen the end of our unease. I have premonitions
of absolute silence, the smiling baby unknowingly famous.
I have seen your book, and my book, side by side,

boarding a train between now and right now.
I have seen us.

Love me,
like the last train home.

Psalm for the First Light
after Jack Agüeros

Lord,

I have always wanted a woman
to share first light with.

Let her be Puerto Rican, Lord,
with brown eyes and good humor
and lips. O, Lord, let her have lips.

Let her always kiss me
the way shadows kiss dawn.
Let her kiss be the dark streaks
between sunbeams, negative space
that says yes, then no, then yes.

Let her kiss be the thing that separates
wakefulness from dreaming. Let her
kiss like there is no difference.

Lord,

I have always wanted a woman
whose kiss is like the first light.

Lorca, your servant, wrote about this.
Dawn in New York, he called it.

Let her kiss render even Lorca mute,
powerless, a blank page he needs to fill
with bullfights.

Let even first light weep
at its insufficiency.

Poem Ending with Another Letter

I need to apologize
for the information I leave
at your doorstep every morning.

Things like *I was a man*
with borrowed eyes, refusing
to see beauty in others, or myself.

And *Every morning with you*
is a wound healing, a new heart
growing over the end of my death.

Because sometimes I wonder
if you believe me. Wonder
if the stanzas pause too often,

or not often enough. You remind me
I've come far since French Roast.
You call my brain sexy, my lips.

Your thighs in my hands, prayers rising
in moaning postures, moving pictures,
white ribbons.

The only letter left is an open heart,
the one you cracked open with visions
of Grace, truth reshaped by your mouth,

the open door of your apartment,
the curled hair you played with, faith,
unwavering, God, my soul, invincible

to you. Mine is the heart you created,
and still you wonder if you are enough.
If you are a moonlit vow.

Amor,

You are hereby permitted to use possessive pronouns when referring to me: my poet. my love. my heart. my sexy thing. my, my, my, my. Yours.

Take this heart you shaped like a master sculptor, the poem you have rewritten all these months, the novel you hammered into shape.

Take this body in its raging imperfection, a landscape where you sing me into every sunrise, a man without apologies.

Take this mind, this brilliance, this insistence on poems and letters, engaging the world on its own terms again, the place where I keep you perfect, and miraculous, the garden of my belief.

Take this hand, which had been bereft, which knows love and streetlamps on Broadway, the small of your back, your trepidation and mine.

Take everything I am, everything I will be, everything I was and was not, and call it sanctuary, pilgrimage, life. Call me lover, man, privileged.

Say you are in love, or in a patch of strawberries, that you see me in your past life to come. Say I am yours, say it without sighs. Say you want, you want, you want. Say need. Say tomorrow, and every tomorrow. Say today. Say five minutes from now. Say, "Make love to me." Say always. Say forever. Say fearless. Say your heart is mine. Say my heart is yours. I will say it.

Love me everyday like Bustelo in the morning. Love me when I am in the next room, writing. Love me when you are writing. Write. Love me the way I love you, unchanged and uncompromising. Write. Love me inside and outside, love me for lunch. Love me the way your lips love green tea. Write. Love me like ritual. Love me like prayer. Write. Write. Write. Love me like I love you writing, living, climbing to the top of Maslow's hierarchy. Love me because you wrote your own creation story. Love me in every room. Love me in Carnegie Hall. Love me over duck, and wine, and mango. Love me, love me, the way Getz's notes love the air between us.

I am yours for as long as the moon means you. I am yours because you knew it in Brooklyn.

Agua de Beber
after Lisel Mueller and Antonio Carlos Jobim

When the rain comes, a fist unclenches in your lower back.

You smell what earth releases:
heat, light, sun baked into grass and asphalt.

A door opens in your skull.
Your characters dance
when you say dance.
Hotel California plays in your kitchen.

Jobim slips bossa nova
underneath your comforter,
where fear is unwelcome
and sleep approaches like a soft foot.

At five in the morning,
I am love without masks,
air breaking into water at the thunder.

Your rain has come, querida.

Agua de beber.
A vine spreads across the floor.
I trace your lips with a red, ripe strawberry.

The first bite walks with purpose.

Agua de beber, camará.

The second builds cities with your name.

My love is rain, corazón, cando hondo
picking up the pen you dropped,
placing it back on your desk.

Stretch your arms to God.
Sleep.
Dream yourself.
Sleep. Dream of rain.

First Light

Aubade: Dawn Viewed Through the Mask of a Bilevel Positive Airway
Pressure Machine

Thank you, God, for the mechanics of my awakening:

air pushing rhythmically over my synapses;
my pupils, a thousand facets of a diamond;
vision creeping into my brain like water
rushing under my door. Still unsure
if this is my eye's sleeping geometry,
or the sun's first testimony,

the alarm clock pours Corcovado
into our bed, where no fear resides,
and perhaps I am aware, as Lazarus was,
of the interplay of light and consciousness,
a voice sounding me into sudden being.

It is you who transforms this bundle of wires,
straps, plastic mask, and motorized lung, back
into quickened flesh with mind and fingers:
"Amor. You're so cold." And you slip your leg

over mine, and your heat becomes my heat,
and your breath becomes my breath.

Aubade at 12:56pm

The draft in your windows wakes you.
A jazzman reads you D.H. Lawrence,
wishing your waist was muted trumpet,
your moans the notes to Corcovado.

The sun refuses the order to shine, to bathe
your closed eyes in winterglow, the deep
red purpose of your bedroom: I will

compose an ode to the Triboro Bridge,
the dervish upon which the city spins, wishing
I was Miles, playing what is not there.

I will love you at 12:56pm, wake you
open-hearted and magnificent,
thunderstruck stargazer.

I will make love to you because you are a city—

questioning light among descending clouds
orange blanket drifting up, then down,
touching fingers, creator and creation.

Speak softly when you rise: yours
is the kingdom of heaven. Hold me like a hand
at mid-afternoon dreaming the Portuguese words
for stay, forever;

Or, swim with me to the eternal.
Dream me the word in Portuguese
for what we are building.

Aubade: Conjure

And when you do awaken,
there is shining red curtain.
Wood floor, pink pajamas.
Cold marble, toothbrush, and toast,
followed by coffee, followed by email.

No.

Say you dreamed it.
Stay in bed, Amor.

Sleep to conjure a world. You are standing
on a beach engulfed by sudden water.

I was waiting for you on the other side of the country,
a new shoreline to which you will always swim.

Sleep to conjure grace. Stop this day and night.
I am the origin. Which must be you, which is
yes, honor, respect. Sleep is a vow
made under moonlight.

Sleep to conjure cherished ones in a circle
we constructed. Let them hear the news
you dreamed: Wake up, wake up.

Aubade: Departure
after Robert Hayden

Summer is far away.

In your hair, the last stanzas of moon
before coffee.

Love. Notes. This is hard work:

I hate everything about the job
except the check, small mercies
on lined paper: food, rent.

The baby is asleep in the next room.
The baby is not a baby.

You, exquisite, your body unfolding
under sheets, architect of wine and wishbone.

Waking you in a delirium of kisses,
drowning sacred acts of sleep.

Your voice is small at this hour, medicine.

I leave my offering at the stove,
enticements from bed.

We keep each other alive this way.
The man who does not know this is lost.

The lock turns, you are safe.

What do you know, what do you know,
of the houses I have built for us?

Aubade: Arrival

I could almost go there
Just to watch you be seen
I could almost go there
Just to live in a dream
~Norah Jones, "I've Got To See You Again"

Awaken like I did, from a coma. Open your eyes
to an angel worshipping the shape of your lips,
and you will never again mistake the moonlight
for living in a dream. The night, real. Her face,
real, the doubting twist of her eye. She loves you.
Believe her. Come back. Believe that, too.

You won't want to watch, or dream, or go anywhere
she is not. The morning, an exodus of flashbacks:
Her hips and yours in synchronized hallelujah down
in her chair. Fishnets. The foyer's echoed steam.
A man like you would stay and eat all her grapefruit;

relax, Pa, relax. Go when she says go there, stay when
she moans at the touch of your hand to her back.
There are so many oceans left to be dreamed, to be
washed away in. There are so many coasts to explore.

Even you will arrive eventually.
She opened her eyes when you made love.
She gifted you the overture to a perfect symphony.

She remembers you, your mouth, your rhythm.
She loves you like a dream worth waking to. She is not

asleep, or even waiting for you. Or even an angel.

Aubade: Departure #2

Your voice at my ear, *I love*

the way you fuck me. Fuck me. Describe
strawberries for breakfast. Every seed
another dawn.

It is raining pineapple juice and Bustelo.
Slide up, slide down. I am inside you,
like a strawberry. *You've got to leave.*

I've got to leave:

before your body exploding, before
my body floating across your lawn,
put your face to my face. Put your eyes
to my eyes. Listen.

Aubade: Admonitions to Her Overeager Lover, Waiting in Bed at 5am

You will want to make love to me
the moment I turn the key. Resist.

You know I have my rituals.
I can't crash into you.

My senses teem with mathematics,
characters dancing across my brain,
dissolving, fading in.

Poet, you have only begun to touch the sound
of my nights, my brain creating. I've only
now stopped moving. I do not need you, yet.

When every synapse chants down first light
with now, I must first coax my body from leaping
the cliff of waking, sit with my prayers, recite
the spell to uncoil the springs in my neck.

To smile at this: This is the life I have chosen
to fly toward, my daughter's reflection
in every mirror I will ever own.

I must choose the honest note,
to the detriment of all arms shaped like surrender.

You must wait. You must close your eyes and dream,
not of the lights of Rio, but the embers of the next room over.
You must send a kiss by text message and relinquish
your curtain's red impatience.

You must harmonize. Amor, listen. I am the one singing.
Did you forget, Amor, that this is my morning song?

Let me choose the notes, like a new ritual unfolding.
Like a poem, Poet, that writes you.

Ars Poetica

1

His life is chancletas and newspapers,
ritual tostadas, enough coffee to wake
every dead abuelo between Vieques and Boquerón.

To understand what this means,
his ears escape to *por la montaña venimos*
pa' invitarnos a comer,
on the west side of an island
he did not grow up in.

To understand what this means,
Viejitas grab their husband's asses,
que pa' eso bebe, pa' eso

To understand what this means,
he thinks of home.
He thinks of Home Depot.

She slips him a caña smile, a cafetaso smile,
a smile *pa' que tu sepas. Tu mujer te 'sta esperando,*
nene. *No jodas,* he ain't ready,

but he's more old school than he thought,
asi que fuck it, he loves her anyway.

2

She dreams color.
She dreams Williamsburg before aging hipsters.
She dreams the Eagles unplugged on the soundtrack.
She dreams cruel worlds and a daughter who tames them.
She dreams dark chocolate hazelnut ridiculous kiss.
She dreams thousands of keyboards and fingers.
She dreams home, friends, Amor, wine, and laughter.
She dreams one minute longer.
She dreams Tuscany.
She dreams abuela's smile.
She dreams me when she's not looking.
She dreams in bossa nova,
She dreams family in every frame.
She dreams peace, peace, peace.
She dreams the greca's elixir every morning.
She dreams sand.
She dreams grass.
She dreams a stamped passport.
She dreams cuatro nights.
She dreams quenepa trees.
She dreams a wall of books, a ladder.
She dreams Boquerón.
She dreams universes spinning at her fingertips
She dreams ink, and good paper.
She dreams me happy.
She dreams me happy, she dreams,

and I want sleep,

           if sleep is the bridge
           I must cross to her door.

3

they needed no translations,
no one to say need, or now,
or when you are not busy,
spending sweet circumstance
crossing interstate highways,
nothing of convenient yes
or reckless abandon, no rule
to measure their silences by.

a single kiss after breakfast,
four hours' sleep, waking up
or not, a talent for dreaming,
poems for every hour apart,
laughter between each breath,
each breath more swift, each
moment more desperate, his
mouth, a strawberry patch.

4

Moonlight fills the passenger seat, a city
is spread before him, a feast of love and light
his eyes were hardly ready for. The shoreline is
dotted orange, the city is asleep under a blanket
of stars crashed to earth, and in the distance,
the bridges he desires to cross, the streets he has
yet to love, steel and stone, quick and slow,
man-made and waterborne. Her avatar
has risen to cast its million names across the river,
bright and brilliant as her face in Williamsburg. This
is the city he would level for her, rebuild in her
mirrors. From under the false promise of electric
shimmer, deep beneath the scurry of the West
Side Highway, his heart is pushing toward the
asphalt, the grim face of old New York. From this
cliff, heaven turns its face to Cancer's mother,
beats a new rhythm into him. The city is a lung.
He is breath. She is pulse.

5

He ventures no guesses as to the nature of her lips
except to say that no simile will describe how
far downriver he has floated upon kissing them. She
wishes him water, more still than the delirium of his
bed, a more peaceful habit than losing sleep or
reacquainting himself with night's blue cloak. She
may as well wish him the cliff under which he writes
her this poem, or the four geese floating
toward the Tappan Zee. They could follow him home,
the birds, the stone, share his bed with the words,
that is, the stars aligning to the whims
of a full moon, in whose service his tides move
for her. He accepts these gifts, in place
of the natural order of things, in place of sleep
and closed fists. In turn, he sets the stone to float
downriver, to the city of his love's love,
and soars over your house on the backs
of geese. The stone, he has left at the shore,
like his old life. He wants to spend the next three
hours sitting outside her door, devising the worst
metaphors for the kiss that has brought him here.
He wants to tear open the reality of water
to describe her heart. He wants to fail, miserably.

6

I want nothing.

Stand in front of me and smile like the sunrise you
never asked for.

You were the cup from which I poured out
the end of never.

I am the page from which you cannot be
erased.

Write yourself.

Use the pen that most loves your hand.

Let there be no breaks in your prose until the story
is ready to end.

Let the story never end.

Let there be shelves of us left behind,
perfectly disordered volumes.

Love, like this.

Love yourself in your darkest days.

You break open like an egg.

Teach me how to unbreak.

I love you purely.
Love my imperfect, body.

Night is the grave I rose from the day I loved you at dawn.

7

Sometimes there is too much to know. There is
a sign that points out what lies on the other side of
this river: other points, bodies of water, boundaries
drawn centuries ago. The shape of land, the current
sweeping mud south, the color of water and clouds.
Someone must have seen this. Someone must have
seen the vista from this cliff and dropped her jaw
in disbelief. There was a poem in her ears. Querida,
there is a poem in your ears. I read it every time
you give it voice and song. You say I am loved, and
I believe you. You say I am the man who sees the city
in one brilliant piece, a unified field you can get
lost in. As I have. Pure love is the water between cliffs,
the slow moving of stone to the right course. The
city is a series of choices to build, and stand perfectly
still. Millions of yes's to each point of light
on the spectrum of the shoreline. I know your yes
like breath. It covers my sky with stars. It reflects
the city's knowing. When you say yes, I want, I need,
come meet me at this cliff. Let me draw
this skyline from memory, on your lips.

8

A night like this will pass without sleep, and she
is the first and last thought—

at a keyboard, a notebook, a soft soundtrack
coaxing the players keeping time

in her stories. She will not tell
her mind to play another's game.

She will give no coin to the organ grinder,
color her world unfamiliar. She has things,

things, things, always, but they will wait
their turn while she reads Erich Fromm.

She wakes precisely at 12:56. One perfect cup
of Bustelo. The laugh only she knows,

the one she keeps to herself when she
says yes, and the universe bends to you.

She is the bridge between climax and denouement,
sleeping between the pages of books, surrounded

by handwritten notes, and no one is answering
the door until she gives place to what is

intertwining itself in her fingers, that is,
she is the architect of stars this night

and every night, adoration is adoration when she
says it is, and she has always been Amor.

This is how you love her. This is how you will lose
your sleep, why you will never be the well

into which she drops her voice.

9

A man with vision needs
salsa music and the sun, in that order.

When you know this,
every poem you write is prophecy,
every dream is shaped
like your brother's smile, every song,

hers. The Upper West Side
has always held your secret,
and when you pass the
place you first held her hand,

where you knew without being told,
where every streetlight washed you in gold,
the tears do not come the way

you expected. Instead, your
heart opens, there is chocolate
in your hand before you realize
home is never the place

you expected. You saw the sun again.
It's the one that led you
from yourself into her blue shoreline.
There is nothing supernatural about saying

your heart travels from dream to dream
to dream. She has sung you
into existence. Love is the only poem
that ever needed to be written.

All this you saw today,
driving with the roof open
on 81st Street and Broadway,
while you were sipping coffee
elsewhere, when she appeared
in the passenger seat of your car,

moving to the song, the radio
that said *mi corazón es suyo.*

10

Love, you:

The corner of your mouth.
The sigh and downward cast eye,
watching me, knowing.
A cup of Bustelo at the balcony,
Mayagüez at your nostrils.
Four generations living.
Five smooth stones inherited mother to mother,
daughter to daughter.
Tomboy with a bike bell,
first alarm of your coming.

In the mirror, reflecting her, and her, and her.
Paved roads leading.
Diagnosed girl, grown at 12.
Blue, yellow, green, Oz.
South Bronx fist.
Hard and soft, Two hands,
praying. Sacrifice and sanctified.
Faith. Brought by God,
the rebel in the temple, overthrowing gold.
Friday night jazz aspirations becoming words.

Watching molecules vibrating,
neglecting transformation.
Alchemy.
Empathy.
Carrying your potential in a plastic bag.
The moist earth beneath the topsoil.
Seed regenerating lilies.
Your own good idea.
Written in several notebooks.
Already victorious.
Entering your houses,

and every story is about you, every poem
writes itself to praise your hands,

every unaccepted prophet speaks
in tongues to you, every dream grows
legs and runs to you.
Unbowed voice blooming in response.

Come to me, love me, if you must. But please, stop talking.

11

No, I'm not facing west, September's
skies are not skipping sunlight across
the edges of clouds about to burst. No.
God is squeezing an overripe mango
in his unseen hand, raining sweet
orange into the mouths of the dead.
seated at a lemon tree, my sister
and my mother saw Tia in a red blouse,
walking between names and dates,
and as surely as I can tell you about
mangos in the sky, I know what awaits
me each November. The sun welcomes
my brother home. The Day of the Dead,
who were never dead. My sister's
llanto: *dejame ir, mami, por favor,*
dejame ir. Seven, the number of God,
his favor and grace, my faith reborn.
Your face and my face, pink paper in my
journal. 11th Street. Coffee, trembling
flesh. Mango in your mouth. Am I
sleeping? Kisses on your back. Am I awake?
Yes.

Comprehending

Luquillo

the sun and the moon, in one sky, conspire
to love even the bend in your elbow the day
you float face up in the bay. a grey halo
rings el yunque in rain, kisses your feet.

words write themselves, inexplicably, in the sand.
you read them with new lips. your bones
ache to remind you; you are the son of caguana,
creation story weaved into the green country.

mata siguaraya. of course you dreamed it:
god does not rain on the beach of your childhood
without his reasons. there had to be something.
there had to be a sequence of things not seen

yet evident:
the man who touched the flag around your neck
and asked you about jesus/
your brother, standing behind you/
a carnival/ a casket/ your grandmother's
voice seeping from the wreck/
a prayer on the bay answered.

the woman you used to love,
entering the water.

say, too:

you never knew my heart's limits
until I attempted to cook for you.

your geography intricate, your body
a map to the islands of my true birth.

my humor hid wounds, the evidence
of wounds, in a rainforest. you were
the first to know their masters.
i set these scars to dance for you.

i set them all on fire for you.

everything and everyone until right now
has been prelude. has been silence.
has been a bad idea made flesh.

you were someone i deserved, a word,
something to conjure because you
brought me joy, and grapefruit.

your love was the temple curtain torn in two.
our bed is the holy of holies.
i worshipped at an altar of red mirrors.

there will always be something to do.
someone will always knock, demand entry.
(say to them: don't come back.)

the present is already the past and the future.
i saw you on court street, on main street,
years before you were a tear in my eye.

the things you didn't understand about us

should be translated into spanish
at your earliest possible convenience.

these things should be recited to you,
at dawn, dropped into the well of your ear
like a wish. like a mission statement.

you were the difference between living
and surviving.

The Boy Says Forever to the Girl

and the girl remains skeptical.

The boy would pledge everything he is and has and aspires to from now until the end of time, because he has read these outcomes in fairy tales, stolen the lines and words and made them into something believable, and even though his heart has been lashed to the rocks and left to the salt sea, and still he gives his love sincerely, without fear or stoplights, the girl reminds him that even he will die, and time is not a straight line that stops and starts, but an agreement among the doomed to mark the lines on the earth's face.

On the boy's face, and the girl's face, there is love, they love purely, at the first light, but the boy insists forever and the girl can only smile and stroke the boy's face and love him for wanting to tear up all his calendars and replace them with her skin.

She cannot comprehend how he intends to close his eyes and make her the morning they greet now with kisses and the promise of white ribbons at noon.

He says to her things like Querida, life, and death, and always; he says the word again like he is searching for a cure: Forever. Forever.

Forever. I will love you forever, I am yours forever, I will be here forever. I will walk through fire unblemished if you say it back.

Say it back.

She is strawberry seed, she is closed mouth, she is heart smile, so close.

Say yes, he says.

Forever is a big word, she responds.

And this is how they leave it, this is how she holds him, this is how he leaves a row of kisses on the back of her neck, this is how they finally fall asleep, his hand on her waist, her body the cuatro he never knew he played this well.

Even a closed eye admits some light.

Red is the last color she saw before the morning dissolved into dreaming.

Forever is the last word he breathed before his fingertips began to bloom strawberries.

For six hours, there were no hours, only two windows, and two sunrises separated by miles, the same dream, the same light of the same sun, the same colors visible to the same eyes closing, and the girl and the boy were neither time nor circumstance but energy, were neither created nor destroyed, were never, were always, were today, were tomorrow, were sacred, were electric, were something, were everything, were the same beam of light traveling the same distance together, were love, were God, were courage, were fearless, were green, were a piece, just one piece, of forever.

Mayagüez

the ocean opens its arms, spreads a banquet of green
for eyes to feast upon. your hair danced
in the open window, a brush to paint the cliffs
of our mothers' dreams, our memories years from now.

to love you is to close my eyes, fly like a turtle above the siguaraya,
to bring life to the open mouths of the incredulous,
words to the silent; to awaken the touch of ocean air in the skin
we inherit, yet always deny.

i knew without needing to ask that there is a spirit, a naming,
a knowing passed on from forever to forever that reads me
at your grandmother's doorway, shuffles coffee into our hands,
asks me to translate the five feet of air between mayagüez
and the bronx. i would have hesitated, or stumbled, except
that i already knew this voice. she stepped out behind the train
on a brilliant sunday in brooklyn. she wore a mauve dress.
she stepped into the waters and conjured stars.
she opened a multicolored door.

when we make the turn down the coast,
our beckoning green and perfect names,
i know i heard that voice
say home, amor, we are home
and this is what i knew of you,
a heart's whisper in my ear, the words
in the sand that spell the dawn
of every mountain morning.

your voice rising to resonate with mango trees in the city of being.
dream your feet moving, south.
i am not there.

Comprehending Forever

Forever is a big word. In seventh grade, forever was the punches,
a school bus, Eddie's bare skin, six inches from my face.
I learned to swallow my head, my tears; to bury, silently,
my ears; to distrust my eyes. I am a man now.
Logic is my only ally. Laugh, clown, and watch the world
marvel at how you hold their attention. *Hold him down, Eddie.*
Hold him down. Eyes fixed into years from now. The shower
drain, compound eye staring up. I hold its attention, laugh, know
what my father has buried. I would not see him cry
again until a cold day in spring. I do not know
the day they pinned me down, but I will say April.

You could not know. You always know. Energy. You know his
breath before you see his face. You could not know, yet
we speak about brothers in April, good men and good poems.
Skin tells me there is logic to be uncovered. My ears
lie and show me Eddie's skin again. I want to know
more about the way you breathe, even now. Subtle boldness coaxes
my ear from the soil. Hold him down. I will not
be buried. Hold him. Tomorrow, today, when you see Dooley smile,
I will shed the last skin I was buried in. Vines
blossom across your name, wind around my brain like a river.
November slips you pink paper. I have already loved you.

He swore he would never speak her name. He was seventeen
in April, 1952. A heart takes decades to break, he learned.
When she returned to her husband, he picked up the mantle
he learned at Enrique's feet. In trade school, he built houses,
raised roofs over his siblings' heads, kept the lights on, laughed.
Hers was not the name he married. Hers was the love
he swallowed. Across a new city, other cold Novembers, he tried
to speak at the end of the six train, in Passaic,
on President Street. When his son's heart split, fifty years later,
his voice, wavering: *Forget that I am your father. Speak to
me, the way you speak to the earth. Bury it here.*

I gave you an imperfect hand. You gave me Erich Fromm.
I gave you the answers I knew. You gave me loving,
you made it a practice. I gave you all my heart.
You gave me sleepless nights. I gave you George Orwell. You
gave me George Orwell. I gave you poems. You gave me
the first person perspective, new eyes to see the world in.
Many years ago, I buried my ears, afraid to feel trembling
in my chin, fire on my tongue and feet. I gave
you my faithless fingers. You gave me dreams: a turtle,
siguaraya, the sun and the moon in the same Luquillo sky.
You gave me loving. I gave you loving. We are timeless.

When my father says he would never cry for a woman,
I will remember tonight. The methodical dialing of numbers, low voice
settling into the phone: *¿Mi amor, donde tu estas? Yo estaba
preocupado.* And she's at the door, where she normally is. Boniata,
the love of his life, the whisper at his pillow. Tears
flow from his eyes when he does not know he's being
watched. When he sees his mother, he remembers the bend in
his elbow, which was the bend in hers. He remembers love
before swallowing. He remembers the book in my mother's hand, the
night she said yes: *The Art of Loving* by Erich Fromm.
I have lived this life already. We are timeless, mi Amor.

As I press my tongue to the screen, tasting rain, Jesus—
crucified on the roof of Donaldson Park Apartments—turns His head
from the black sky. This is true. As true as Abuela's
voice in clear August air, my sister surviving the car crash;
as Rogelia's red blouse in the cemetery; as Palla's voice calling:
Ya, ven mi hermana; as Miriam's voice calling: *Dejame ir, mami,*
dejame ir. As Dooley's footsteps in my mother's, my sister's sleepless
nights; as Dooley's smile at the wedding, behind the priest,
the table at which my family gathers each November. I say
true the way you say forever, the faith you taught me
bearing fruit. Say love, where once you could not see strawberries.

Let me drink from your glass. Let grace flood our stomachs.
Let me love everyone you love. The hours I spend with
your names in my mouth. Moongirl. Amor. Querida. Let me love
you like a prayer answered. Let me love you like prayer.
In April my knowing skin reminded me I could not bend
visible light around my body, could not touch forever without dying.
In November, your trembling leg at 5am. The wine was perfect,
and when the swirling finally hit us, when death and life
reassembled our bodies in the dark blue, the barely audible voice
of the first skyline we kissed beneath, silenced itself in deference
to the holy, awaited your sleep to whisper: *Forever, moongirl, Forever.*

I awakened under the stars,
and I was loved.
Stories of physics and time travel
blossomed in your mouth
like the light of a thousand years,
traveled into what I understood
to be my eyes. A star is gravity
and time squeezing energy
into the kisses I freely gave. This
is how I know about transforming,
that love is the only permanent thing,

and the only explanation for why
a day is a year, or a white butterfly.
I was at the edge of the Palisades,
where my soul testified,
and every star carried you
in a thousand year journey to
my fingers, which are this book,
which I now send back into
the vacuum to greet another
stargazer, standing on another shore
in a world I haven't seen yet,

but will. I loved
in a manner unbecoming of the way
the world would prefer me.
I've had time to be alone, to be
cynical and altogether ordinary,
never forgetting the rain, the night,
eleven blocks of a metered city,
running to greet you. I loved
intentionally, in spite of the tears
that said no to 11th Street. Love, stand
still and stare into the sky. Find me.

You always do.

Acknowledgments

Grateful acknowledgment to these editors and their journals, for finding these poems their first homes:

Thrush Poetry Journal, Helen Vitoria, Editor
"Aubade at 12:56pm."

Hanging Loose, Robert Hershon, Editor
"Psalm For the First Light"
"Lullaby"

About the Author

Rich Villar is a writer born and raised in northern New Jersey. A longtime advocate for the Latino/a voice in U.S. letters, he has been quoted on Latino literature and culture by *The New York Times* and *The Daily News*. His work has been featured on NPR's "Latino USA" and in the journals *Hanging Loose, Beltway Poetry Quarterly*, and *Black Renaissance Noire*, among others. He directs Acentos, a grassroots project fostering communities around Latino/a literature.